Florida
The Sunshine State

Tika Downey

PowerKiDS
press™

New York

Published in 2010 by The Rosen Publishing Group, Inc.
29 East 21st Street, New York, NY 10010

First Edition

Editor: Joanne Randolph
Book Design: Greg Tucker
Photo Researcher: Jessica Gerweck

Photo Credits: Cover Lester Lefkowitz/Getty Images; p. 5 © Alan Schein Photography/Corbis; p. 7 © North Wind/North Wind Picture Archives; p. 9 © Kevin Fleming/Corbis; pp. 11, 13, 15, 22 (bird) Shutterstock.com; p. 17 © Douglas Peebles/Corbis; p. 19 © Angelo Cavalli/Robert Harding World Imagery/Corbis; p. 21 Bruce Weaver/Stringer/Getty Images; p. 22 (tree) © www.istockphoto.com/ Marje Cannon; p. 22 (animal) © www.istockphoto.com/Dennis Guyitt; p. 22 (flower) © www.istockphoto.com/Kristen Johansen; p. 22 (Janet Reno and Emmit Smith) Getty Images; p. 22 (Osceola) © CORBIS.

Library of Congress Cataloging-in-Publication Data

Downey, Tika.
  Florida : the Sunshine State / Tika Downey. — 1st ed.
    p. cm. — (Our amazing states)
  Includes index.
  ISBN 978-1-4042-8109-7 (library binding) — ISBN 978-1-4358-3338-8 (pbk.) —
ISBN 978-1-4358-3339-5 (6-pack)
  1. Florida—Juvenile literature. I. Title.
  F311.3.D69 2010
  975.9—dc22
                                             2008055826

Manufactured in the United States of America

Contents

The Sunshine State

Look at a map of the United States. Do you see the state in the bottom right corner that sticks out into the ocean like a pointing finger? That is Florida. It is a peninsula. A peninsula is a piece of land that has water on three sides.

People often think of oranges or orange juice when they think of Florida. The state is famous for its oranges. It is also famous as a great place for vacations. You can visit places such as Disney World or the Everglades. Florida has great weather for vacations, too. It is well known for being sunny almost every day! That is why Florida is called the Sunshine State.

Florida's coastline is more than 8,400 miles (13,500 km) long, with lots of beaches. Only Alaska has a longer coastline.

A Peek at Florida's Past

Did you know that *florida* means "full of flowers" in Spanish? Spanish **explorer** Juan Ponce de León named the peninsula Florida in 1513. He called it this because he arrived around Easter, which the Spanish call *Pascua Florida*, or Easter of the Flowers.

Later Spanish explorers founded St. Augustine in 1565. This was the first lasting European settlement in what is now the United States. Native Americans, who had lived in Florida for over 11,500 years, fought the outsiders. After a long time of fighting, the Europeans won and claimed all the land.

Florida became a U.S. **territory** in 1821. It became the twenty-seventh state on March 3, 1845.

Here Native Americans are shown attacking an American fort during the Second Seminole War. Three Seminole wars were fought in Florida, between 1817 and 1858.

Sand, Sea, and Sun

Florida has mostly low, flat land. Its long coastline has sandy beaches and **swamps**. Its most famous islands, the Florida Keys, are near the state's southern tip. People come from all over the world to swim off Florida's beaches.

Northern Florida has hills, valleys, and forests. Throughout the state, there are rivers and lakes. Lake Okeechobee is Florida's largest and most famous lake.

Florida is almost always warm, even in winter. It is usually sunny, but it has a rainy season that lasts from May to October. Sometimes powerful storms called hurricanes bring heavy rain and strong wind to Florida.

Here a boat motors along in Lake Okeechobee. "Okeechobee" is a Native American word that means "plenty big water."

The River of Grass

South of Lake Okeechobee is one of Florida's most beautiful wild places, the Everglades. Many people think the Everglades is a swamp. In fact, the Everglades is a slow-moving river that flows south from Lake Okeechobee. It is up to 50 miles (80 km) wide but only about 1 foot (30 cm) deep.

The Everglades is often called a river of grass because it is filled with a tall, grasslike plant called saw grass. The river is an important home to many plants, such as the **bald cypress** and **sabal palm**, and animals, such as the pelican, wood stork, and alligator. The Everglades is also home to many **endangered species**, including the Florida panther.

This great blue heron looks for fish in the Everglades. The great blue heron is 4 feet (1 m) tall, though it weighs only 5 pounds (2 kg)!

Wild Florida

You know about Florida's beaches, but did you know that it has huge forests all over the state? These forests are home to many kinds of trees, including cypresses, **mangroves**, and palm, pine, oak, gum, and hickory trees.

Many birds and animals make their homes in Florida. You can see turkeys, pelicans, armadillos, otters, bears, Florida panthers, **manatees**, crocodiles, and the state **reptile**, alligators.

The American alligator can grow to be about 12 feet (4 m) long. Unlike most reptiles, mother alligators guard their eggs and take good care of their babies for about a year after they are born.

The American alligator lives in freshwater marshes, swamps, rivers, and lakes. Hunting mainly at night, these alligators eat a lot of fish, turtles, snakes, and small land animals.

Making Money

Florida's sunny weather is good for growing crops. Did you know that Florida produces about two-thirds of the oranges grown in the United States? Florida's farmers also grow lots of strawberries, blueberries, watermelons, and **sugarcane**. Do you have plants inside your classroom or home? They might have come from Florida, too.

The weather also draws many businesses to Florida. These businesses make everything from orange juice and jellies to computer and airplane parts.

Sunshine also makes Florida a popular vacation spot. About 80 million people visit the state every year! These visitors add more money to the state's **economy** than anything else.

Florida grows many kinds of oranges, including ambersweet, navel, pineapple, and Valencia oranges. More than 10,000 orange growers work in Florida.

Let's Talk About Tallahassee

Tallahassee has been the capital since 1824. It is in northwestern Florida. Its name comes from a Native American word meaning "old town."

Native Americans lived there centuries ago. Spanish explorer Hernando de Soto camped there in 1539, but the first Spanish settlement was not formed there for nearly another hundred years.

You can learn about Florida's history at the Tallahassee Museum of History and Natural Science and the Museum of Florida History. You can also visit the remains of an old Indian village. If you like forests, you can also go to the Apalachicola National Forest.

This is Tallahassee's historic capitol, which houses a research center and museum. The tall building behind it is the new capitol building.

Welcome to Disney World

Have you heard of Disney World? It has been one of Florida's most popular places to visit since it opened in 1971.

Disney World has two water parks and four **theme parks**, the Magic Kingdom, Epcot, Disney's Hollywood Studios, and Disney's Animal Kingdom. The Magic Kingdom has rides, and workers there dress as Disney characters, such as Mickey Mouse. At Epcot, visitors learn about different countries, cultures, and new technology. Hollywood Studios is based on Disney movies and lets visitors become part of the action. Animal Kingdom is a large zoo with all sorts of interesting animals.

The Magic Kingdom is Disney World's most popular park. About 17 million people visit it every year!

Wild Sights and Bright Lights

Visitors to Florida can see wild places, busy cities, and everything in between. You can visit the forests, the Everglades, or Florida's beautiful beaches. Shark Valley, in the Everglades, is a place where you can see alligators and other Everglades animals up close. John Pennekamp **Coral Reef** State Park, in the Keys, is a fun park where you can see reefs firsthand.

You can also visit Miami, a big city with lots of things to do. In St. Augustine, you can see buildings that are centuries old. At the John F. Kennedy Space Center, you can learn about space travel. If you visit Florida, what would you like to see?

Glossary

bald cypress (BALD SY-pruhs) A large tree with needle-shaped leaves that fall off in autumn.

coral reef (KOR-ul REEF) An underwater hill of coral.

economy (ih-KAH-nuh-mee) The way in which a country, state, or business oversees its supplies and power sources.

endangered species (in-DAYN-jerd SPEE-sheez) Kinds of animals that will probably die out if people do not keep them safe.

explorer (ek-SPLOR-ur) Someone who travels and looks for new land.

manatees (MA-nuh-teez) Large air-breathing animals that live in warm ocean waters and eat ocean plants.

mangroves (MAN-grohvz) Trees that grow in swamps and along rivers.

reptile (REP-tyl) A cold-blooded animal that has lungs and scales.

sabal palm (SAY-buhl PALM) A tall palm tree with fan-shaped leaves that grows widely in Florida.

sugarcane (SHUH-gur-kayn) A type of grass that has sugar juice in its stems.

swamps (SWOMPS) Wet land with a lot of trees and bushes.

territory (TER-uh-tor-ee) Land that is controlled by a person or a group of people.

theme parks (THEEM PARKS) Parks with rides and other things to do that are based on one main idea.

Florida State Symbols

State Tree
Sabal Palm

State Animal
Florida Panther

State Flag

State Bird
Mockingbird

State Flower
Orange Blossom

State Seal

Famous People from Florida

Osceola
(1804–1838)
Born in Alabama
(moved to Florida 1814),
Seminole War Chief

Janet Reno
(1938–)
Born in Miami, FL
Attorney General

Emmitt Smith
(1969–)
Born in Pensacola, FL
Football Player

Florida State Map

Legend

○ Major City

⭐ Capital

∿ River

Pensacola

⭐ Tallahassee

Jacksonville

St. Augustine

Gainesville

St. Marys River

Lake George

Daytona Beach

St. Johns River

Orlando

Cape Canaveral

Kissimmee River

Tampa

St. Petersburg

Lake Okeechobee

Caloosahafchee River

Fort Myers

Fort Lauderdale

Naples

The Everglades

Miami

The Florida Keys

Florida State Facts

Population: 18,251,243

Area: 58,560 square miles (151,670 sq km)

Motto: "In God We Trust"

Song: "Swanee River" ("Old Folks at Home")
by Stephen C. Foster

Index

Web Sites

Due to the changing nature of Internet links, PowerKids Press has developed an online list of Web sites related to the subject of this book. This site is updated regularly. Please use this link to access the list:

www.powerkidslinks.com/amst/fl/